Gluten-Free Baking Cookbook

Delicious and Healthy, 100% Gluten-Free
Cake & Bake Recipes You Will Love

By Kira Novac (ISBN: 978-1-80095-041-2)

Copyright ©Kira Novac 2015

www.amazon.com/author/kira-novac

Table of contents

Introduction

Dear Reader,

Thank you so much for taking an interest in my book. It really means a lot to me. I have created it to show you a myriad of ways to make a gluten-free diet enjoyable, tasty, sweet and fun. Included are the best of my gluten-free dessert recipes including cakes, cookies, and puddings plus other delicious gluten-free treats. I can guarantee that your family will love them!

Aside from the actual recipes, I included the food list for your quick reference as well as the basic information about a gluten-free lifestyle. I totally understand what it's like to find out that you (or a family member) can't tolerate gluten and must eat a gluten-free diet. You think: *What? No rice, no bread, no pasta, no cookies, no cakes? What the heck can I enjoy?* What's even worse is that many products are marketed as healthy and gluten-free but in fact are processed and full of chemicals. This is why the best tip I can give you is that you take action and get started on healthy, gluten-free baking. Your family will love you for that! All the recipes presented in this book were tested on my friends and family (aged from 4 to 87) and they all enjoyed them. Moreover, gluten-free cakes do not make you feel heavy and there are no digestive issues that you may have after eating gluten contain foods.

Why Gluten-Free?

It seems as though a new fad diet hits the newsstands every couple of weeks. Some celebrity is always coming out with a new secret to staying skinny and nutritionists debate the merits of the most recent cleanse or detox. The gluten-free diet is by no means new, but it has become newly popularized over the last decade or so. Many people switch to this diet under the misguided impression that it will help them to magically lose weight while others simply make the switch to follow the latest trend. Before you switch to the popular gluten-free diet, you should take a moment to learn the basics about this diet including its benefits, risks, and what exactly the diet entails.

My name is Kira and I am a 35-year-old mother of one. A few years ago my son was diagnosed with celiac (also called celiac sprue) disease and, while the diagnosis came as a bit of a shock, I am glad to finally have an answer to my son's health problems. When my son was diagnosed I made the decision to not only provide him with the gluten-free diet he needed, but to create a healthy lifestyle for myself and my entire family. We have never really been a fast food family, but I am ashamed to admit that frozen desserts and take-out appeared on our weekly menu more often than they should have. Now, however, I am committed to cooking for my family several times a week and we have all made the switch to the gluten-free diet for the benefit of my son. Gluten-free baking is definitely one of our favorite rituals and I can't wait to share my recipes with you.

This type of diet has a number of benefits even for people without celiac disease and those without gluten sensitivities. Many people suffer from a condition called gluten intolerance and they do not even realize it - switching to the gluten-free diet can completely transform their lives. Removing gluten from your diet can help to improve and regulate your digestion and it may provide relief from mood disorders and problems with concentration. We all need focus, energy and better concentration, right? Each person reacts to the gluten-free diet differently but I am a firm believer that it can be a useful tool if you want to improve your health and transform your life.

Committing to the gluten-free diet is not easy and it isn't a decision you should take lightly. If you are thinking about making the switch it is my hope that this book will provide you with the information you need in order to make a well-informed decision. If you do decide that the gluten-free diet is right for you, you will find a collection of delicious dessert recipes in this book that I have created for my family and am now sharing with you. Try a few recipes to see how you like them and you might be surprised just how easy it is to switch to the gluten-free diet.

If you are ready to learn more about this diet and how it can benefit you, turn the page and keep reading!

Free Complimentary Recipe eBook

Thank you so much for taking an interest in my work!

As a thank you, I would love to offer you a free complimentary recipe eBook to help you achieve vibrant health. It will teach you how to prepare amazingly tasty and healthy gluten-free treats so that you never feel deprived or bored again!

As a special bonus, you will be able to receive all my future books (kindle format) for free or only $0.99.

Download your free recipe eBook here:

http://bit.ly/gluten-free-desserts-book

About the Gluten-Free Diet

Before you decide whether or not the gluten-free diet is the right choice for you, you need to learn everything you can about the diet. The gluten-free diet is more than just another fad diet – it is intended to be a lifestyle choice and one that many people follow out of medical necessity. The gluten-free diet is quite simple – it is a diet that is completely free from gluten-containing foods. In order to understand the gluten-free diet, you first need to understand what gluten is and where it comes from.

What is Gluten?

Gluten is a type of protein composite and it is commonly found in certain grains including wheat, barley, rye, and triticale (a hybrid form of wheat). Gluten is actually a composite made up of two storage proteins – glutenin and gliadin – which are joined with a starch. This protein composite is found in the endosperm of several grass-like grains and it is what gives bread dough its elasticity, rise, and chewy texture. Gluten can be found in a wide variety of different foods because it is found in wheat flour and it is commonly used to thicken liquid foods like soups and sauces.

On its own, gluten is not necessarily bad – it is primarily bad for people who have celiac disease or other gluten-related conditions like allergies, intolerance, or sensitivity. It is estimated that about 1 in 133 people have celiac disease, an autoimmune disease exacerbated by the consumption of gluten, and that millions of people suffer from some kind of gluten-related intolerance or sensitivity. It is also estimated that about 99% of people who suffer from problems related to gluten aren't even aware of it because the symptoms of gluten intolerance or sensitivity overlap with the symptoms of many other diseases.

Why is Gluten Bad?

Again, gluten is not necessarily bad but it can cause problems for those people who suffer from certain conditions including celiac disease and gluten intolerance or sensitivity. The symptoms of celiac disease vary greatly from one person to another which makes it very difficult to diagnose. In some individuals with celiac disease gluten causes digestive issues like diarrhea, gas, or bloating. In others, however, it causes fatigue, brain fog, weight loss, anxiety, depression, as well as a number of other mental/behavioral symptoms.

Celiac disease is actually an autoimmune condition, though many people mistakenly believe it is a type of allergy. When a person with celiac disease consumes gluten, their body regards the gluten protein as a foreign invader and produces an immune response. In addition to targeting the gluten, however, the immune cells end up attacking healthy cells in the small intestine as well. As a result, the villi lining the small intestine become damaged and it may result in the malabsorption of nutrients – this is likely the cause of certain celiac disease-related symptoms like chronic fatigue.

Gluten intolerance is a completely different condition. While individuals with celiac disease experience an immune response when they consume gluten, individuals with gluten intolerance typically experience gastrointestinal symptoms like diarrhea, bloating, gas, and abdominal pain. Celiac disease is similar to an extreme form of gluten intolerance but it is possible to have a gluten intolerance without having celiac disease. The only treatment for either condition is to follow a gluten-free diet.

In individuals with celiac disease or gluten intolerance/sensitivity, consuming gluten can result in a number of serious problems including the following:

- Gut inflammation
- Autoimmune response
- Premature cell death and oxidation
- Leaky gut syndrome
- Bacterial overgrowth in the intestinal tract
- Vitamin D deficiency

For these reasons, it is very important that individuals diagnosed with celiac disease, gluten intolerance, and/or gluten sensitivity completely remove gluten from their diets. This is the only proven treatment that will result in relief from symptoms.

Gluten-Containing Foods

Switching to the gluten-free diet can be tricky because gluten is found in so many foods. Not only is it found in baked goods made from wheat and other gluten-containing grains, but it is also commonly found in other foods like fried foods, Asian-style sauces, soups, beer, snack foods, cereals, and more. Fortunately, most food labels for commercially-produced foods carry an allergy statement which will tell you if the product contains wheat. There are some ingredients, however, in which gluten can be hiding that you may not suspect.

For example, anything with "malt" in the ingredients is typically made from barley and is therefore not gluten-free. Breaded meats, commercial sauces, thickened soups, and most beer is also not gluten-free. Even oats, which are technically gluten-free, can be contaminated by coming into contact with wheat grains during processing. Below you will find a list of common foods that typically contain gluten:

- Spelt
- Wheat
- Kamut
- Triticale
- Durum
- Einkorn
- Farina
- Semolina
- Cake flour
- Matzo
- Couscous
- Barley
- Rye
- Bread
- Pastries
- Breakfast cereal
- Cakes and pies

- Bagels and biscuits
- Muffins
- Pizza dough
- Pumpernickel
- Malt beverages
- Malt syrup
- Malt flavoring
- Malt powder
- Malt vinegar
- Beer
- Blue cheese
- Processed cheese
- Seasoning mixes
- Soups
- Sauces
- Soy sauce
- Teriyaki sauce
- Licorice
- Imitation crab meat
- Self-basting turkey
- Non-dairy creamer
- Sausages
- Hot dogs
- Stuffing mixes
- Pretzels
- Snack bars

• Snack mixes

The list above is not exhaustive, but it will give you a good idea what type of foods and products typically contain gluten.

Gluten-Free Foods

Looking at the list from the last section, you might be wondering what foods are left. Though it is true that gluten is found in a wide variety of different foods, most unprocessed foods are naturally gluten-free. This includes things like fresh fruits, vegetables, herbs, nuts, seeds, eggs, meats, and oils. Most dairy products aside from malted milk, blue cheese, and certain flavors of yogurt and ice cream are also free from gluten-containing ingredients.

As an alternative to gluten-containing flours like all-purpose flour and wheat flour there are many flours made from nuts or non-gluten-containing grains that you can use to make gluten-free versions of your favorite recipes. Below you will find a list of gluten-free flours and baking substitutes:

• Amaranth flour

- Arrowroot powder
- Almond flour
- Baking powder
- Baking soda
- Buckwheat flour
- Chestnut flour
- Chia seed flour
- Coconut flour
- Corn flour
- Cornstarch
- Garbanzo bean flour
- Ground flaxseed
- Hazelnut flour
- Mesquite flour
- Millet flour
- Oat flour
- Potato flour
- Potato starch
- Soy flour
- Tapioca flour
- Tapioca starch
- Quinoa flour
- Rice flour
- Sorghum flour
- Teff flour
- Xanthan gum

In fact, you can make your own gluten-free flour blends to use in your favorite recipes. To make a gluten-free flour blend, simply combine equal parts of two different gluten-free flours with an equal portion of a gluten-free starch. Most gluten-free flours and starches will work well with this ratio except for almond flour and potato flour.

Avoiding Cross-Contamination

When you make the switch to the gluten-free diet you need to do more than just avoid gluten-containing ingredients – you also need to avoid cross-contamination. This is especially important for individuals with celiac disease because they may have a reaction to even the smallest amount of gluten. Cross-contamination happens when a food that is gluten-free comes into direct or indirect contact with a food or ingredient that contains gluten. This can happen during the manufacturing process for commercial foods or in your very own kitchen. If you do not plan on having your entire family make the switch to the gluten-free diet, you may need to keep two different containers of certain products like peanut butter, jams/jellies, and butter to make sure that cross-contamination isn't a problem.

When eating out on the gluten-free diet it is important that you let your server and the cook know about your dietary restrictions. Many recipes offer gluten-free items on their menus but you still need to be sure that they take precautions against cross-contamination. For example, your dish needs to be prepared with clean utensils in a pot or pan that hasn't come into contact with gluten-containing ingredients. Some restaurants even keep separate utensils and cookware for use in preparing gluten-free menu items.

While the gluten-free diet is rapidly gaining in popularity, many people still have a poor understanding of the diet. This being the case, you need to be very careful when you go out to eat. You may even want to call the restaurant ahead of time and speak to the manager to make sure that they can accommodate your dietary restrictions. Do not assume that everyone knows what celiac disease is, or even what gluten is, and do not hesitate to educate people when necessary to make sure that you do not become a victim of cross-contamination.

Risks Associated with the Gluten-Free Diet

As is true for any diet, switching to the gluten-free diet does come with certain risks. Individuals who follow gluten-free diets have been known to exhibit lower than normal levels of certain vitamins and minerals including iron, fiber, calcium, thiamin, niacin, riboflavin, and folate. Ask your doctor about supplements and always be sure to check with him before making any changes to your diet. Once you switch over to the gluten-free diet (especially if you have celiac disease or a gluten intolerance/sensitivity), your body may produce severe reactions if you accidentally ingest a little gluten. The longer you follow the gluten-free diet without deviation, the more severe your reaction will be in cases like this. Even if you do not experience physical symptoms after eating gluten, it could still be doing damage to your intestines.

Because the gluten-free diet has become more popular of late, gluten-free versions of many processed foods are becoming more widely available. Of course, these foods are often much more expensive than the regular version with some products costing double (or more) the price of the traditional version. Many people who switch to the gluten-free diet without doing their research (especially those who don't have a medical necessity for following the diet) do not realize that gluten-free versions of processed foods are still processed foods – they can still be high in calories, fat, and sugar. Just because something is gluten-free doesn't necessarily make it healthy. You still need to monitor your calorie intake on a gluten-free diet and make healthy food choices such as portion control.

If you suffer from celiac disease or have a gluten intolerance/sensitivity, switching to the gluten-free diet may not be choice – it could be a medical necessity. Even those who do not have a medical need to follow the diet can still benefit from removing gluten-from their diet, however. If you are considering switching to the gluten-free diet, take the information from this chapter to heart and talk to your doctor before making the switch. If you decide that the gluten-free diet is indeed the right choice for you, give some of the recipes in this book a try!

Gluten-Free Baking Recipes

Amazingly Sweet Banana Cupcake w/ Cream Cheese Frosting

Bananas are jam-packed with nutrients and can also give your desserts an amazing flavor. Sugar is optional in this recipe; you can very well do without it. However, if you do decide to use sugar, make sure it's cane sugar or stevia powder.

Bananas are an excellent source of magnesium that helps us have more energy and concentrate better.

Total Cooking Time: 58m
Prepping Time: 20m
Cooking Time: 28m
Cool Time: 10m
Serving Size: 7

Ingredients

- ½ cup butter (or coconut oil)
- 1½ cup cane sugar
- 2 organic eggs (free-range)
- ¼ cup almond milk (unsweetened, organic)
- Baking soda (1 teaspoon)

- 1¼ cup white rice flour
- ¾ cup tapioca flour
- 1 teaspoon xanthan gum
- 3 large bananas, mashed
- 1 teaspoon vanilla extract

Cream Cheese Frosting

- 4 tablespoon cream cheese or coconut cream
- 4 tablespoon coconut oil
- 4 tablespoons sugar (cane sugar or stevia are my recommendations)
- 2-3 tablespoons of coconut milk (you can also use almond milk, make sure it's organic)
- 1 teaspoon of vanilla extract

Directions

1. To get the baking party started, pre-heat oven to 350 degrees F.
2. In the meantime, combine butter (or coconut oil) with sugar. Mix until creamy and fluffy.
3. Now add eggs. Combine baking soda, white rice flour, tapioca flour and xanthan gum in a separate mixing bowl.
4. Alternate between adding tablespoons of flour mix and milk to the sugar mixture. Stir with every alternation.
5. Beat until dough is fully mixed.

6. Add liners to cupcake tray and sprits each cupcake with oil spray.
7. Fill ¾ of the liner with batter. Bake for 24-28minutes
8. Let cupcake cool.

Finally

Combine cream cheese and butter in a bowl and whisk until soft. Add sugar, vanilla extract and coconut or almond milk. Whisk slowly until creamy and fluffy. Ice cupcakes with frosting.

Mystery Black Forest Cake

While this recipe calls for cherries, you could also experiment and use blackberries or strawberries. I always make sure I serve this cake with some fruit to make sure there is some vitamin party going on! It's easier to make your kids interested in eating fruit if you serve it with a yummy cake (that is all natural and gluten-free).

Start embracing a gluten-free life today!

Total Cooking Time: 4hr 50m
Prepping Time: 60m
Cooking Time: 50
Cool Time: 3hr
Serving Size: 10

Ingredients

Cherry Filling

- 16 ounce frozen maraschino cherries, thawed
- 2 tablespoons of cherry liqueur
- ⅓ cup sugar (cane or stevia)
- 2 tablespoons cornstarch

Cake

- 1 cup of unsalted organic butter
- 1/4 cup of cocoa powder (raw)
- 1/4 cup of cream (or coconut cream)
- 1 cup of dark chocolate
- 5 large organic eggs
- 1/4 cup cane sugar or stevia powder

Frosting

- 1 14-ounce can of coconut cream
- 4 tablespoons stevia powder
- ½ tsp vanilla (extracted)
- 1cup dark chocolate chopped

Directions

1. Chill coconut cream in the fridge overnight.
2. Make sure coconut cream is in an area of the fridge where it will not be moved.
3. Place large mixing bowl in freezer.
4. Drain thawed cherries and reserve cherry juice.
5. Blend your cherry juice with: cherry liqueur, cornstarch and sugar.

6. Cook over medium heat, whisk for about 10 minutes.

7. Cool the mixture and then add the cherries. You may have to fold them into the syrup. Refrigerate until cool and thick.

8. Heat oven to 350 degrees F. Prep two 8 inch round pans with butter.

9. Heat the butter at a low heat.

10. Add 1/4 cup of cream.

11. Stir energetically.

12. Add the chocolate and stir well until it melts down.

13. Remove from heat.

14. In medium mixing bowl, whisk: eggs, sugar and cocoa.

15. Whisk in the chocolate.

16. Once the batter is smooth, transfer it to the prepped pans and bake for 45 to 50 minutes.

17. Then simply cool down for about 1 hour.

18. Remove the coconut cream from the fridge slowly and carefully so cream will remain intact. Scoop the thick, creamy part off the top.

19. Place cream in your chilled mixing bowl. Whisk for 30 seconds until creamy. Now add vanilla extract and stevia powder.

20. Mix until super smooth mixture is achieved. Refrigerate immediately.

21. Enrich the surface of the cake with a thin layer of whipped coconut cream.

22. Add chilled cherry filling and spread evenly along coconut cream filling.

23. Chill the cake so that the coconut cream is firm.

Final steps

1. Lightly place the other 8-inch round chocolate cake on top of the prepped cake.

2. Spread a thick layer of coconut cream on the surface of the double layered cake.

3. Completely cover cake with cream filling including the sides of the cake.

4. Cool the cake until coconut cream is firm. Scoop the rest of the cherry filling on its top.

5. Grate the dark chocolate over the top.

6. Serve.

7. Good news, you can make some more and store it as it will refrigerate for even up to 14 days! (The problem is that is disappears very quick...I wonder who is to blame...)

Carrot Cake

This is one of our favorite gluten-free and guilt-free treats. It can even make a great breakfast (you can serve it with some fruits or home-made marmalade).

You can also transform the recipe into a spicy carrot bread. Simply use more salt, don't use sugar, and add spices like curry and black pepper. Your imagination is the only limit of what can be done.

Total Cooking Time: 2h 10m
Prepping Time: 15m - 20m
Cooking Time: 40m – 50m
Cool Time: 1h
Serving Size: 20

Ingredients

Cake

- 1 ¼ cups vegetable oil
- 5 large organic eggs
- 1/2 cup sugar (I recommend cane or stevia)
- 1tablespoon ground cinnamon
- ½ teaspoon ginger (powdered)

- ¼ teaspoon cloves (powdered)
- 1 teaspoon salt (I recommend Himalayan salt)
- ¼ cup white rice flour
- ¼ cup tapioca flour
- ½ cup potato starch
- 1 ½cup brown rice flour
- 2 teaspoons baking soda
- ½ teaspoon xanthan gum
- 3 ½ cups carrots (grated)
- 1 ½ cups walnuts, chopped

Frosting

- ½ cup coconut cream
- Pinch Himalayan salt
- 1 teaspoon vanilla (extract)
- ½ cup stevia powder

Directions

1. Heat oven to 350 degrees F. Butter 10 inch bundt pan.
2. Mix the oil, eggs, sugar, cinnamon, ginger, cloves and salt.

3. In a separate bowl, mix in the white rice flour, tapioca flour, potato starch, brown rice flour, baking soda and xanthan gum.

4. Mix ingredients until fully blended.

5. Combine the two mixtures (sugar and flour).Blend until batter is completely combined.

6. Fold in the carrots and walnuts until it is blended fully.

7. Now slowly and carefully pour your batter into the prepped bundt pan.

8. Simply bake for about45 minutes.

While cake is baking make frosting:

1. Mix all the frosting ingredients.

2. Beat until smooth.

3. Add salt, stevia and vanilla.

4. Let sit for 5 minutes.

Final steps

1. Remove cake from the oven.

2. Cool cake for 5 minutes.

3. Then, place onto a tray.

4. Cool for another 25 minutes before frosting.

Frost the cake with a spatula. Let sit for another 10 minutes so that frosting can set.

Smells delicious, right? Enjoy and eat to your heart's content. It's simply irresistible!

Chocolate Brownie

Cocoa powder is an excellent healthy alternative to chocolate.

What I love about a gluten-free diet lifestyle is that it helps you leave your comfort zone and look for healthier alternatives. I used to be very set in my ways and thought that all this "healthy stuff" was just a "weird food". However, now it's normal food to me. Moreover, it tastes delicious. Find out yourself! Nothing can beat chocolate brownies...Personally I love to serve them with some almond milk or green tea. Yummy and healthy!

Total Cooking Time: 1h 30m
Prepping Time: 40m (-12m)
Cooking Time: 42m
Cool Time: 20m
Serving Size: 24

Ingredients

- 7 ounces dark cocoa organic chocolate, chopped
- 8 tablespoons butter
- 1/2 cup sugar (brown, cane or stevia)
- 3 large organic eggs
- 2 teaspoon pure vanilla extract

- 1/8 cup white flour
- 1/8 cup tapioca flour
- ¼ cup potato starch
- ¾cup brown rice flour
- 1 teaspoon xanthan gum
- 2 tablespoons cocoa powder
- 1 teaspoon Himalayan salt
- ½ teaspoon baking powder

Directions

1. To get the super healthy and totally gluten free baking party started, pre-heat oven to350 degrees F.
2. Place aluminum foil both on the bottom and sides of a 9 inch by13 inch baking pan.
3. Pour an inch of water into a saucepan let it simmer.
4. Set a heatproof bowl in the opening of the pot.
5. Make sure the water doesn't touch the bottom of the bowl so it doesn't melt the bowl.
6. Add chocolate to the bowl.
7. Stir until chocolate is soft.
8. Add butter.
9. Stir mixture.
10. Now remove from heat and add in brown sugar (or other sugar of your choice) until it is dissolved.

11. Stir in eggs and vanilla until completely incorporated.

Final steps

1. Prepare another bowl.
2. Now whisk: white flour, tapioca flour, potato starch, brown rice flour, as well as: xanthan gum, cocoa powder, sea salt and baking powder.
3. Once flour mixture is completely combined slowly stir into the melted chocolate mixture until each mixture is fully mixed.
4. Spread evenly into prepped pan.
5. Bake for 20minutes.
6. Cool for 10 minutes.

Chocolate Cake with Coconut Flour

Coconut flour is a must but for any gluten-free diet fun. It will help you transform traditional recipes into healthier, gluten-free ones. Coconut flour is also paleo diet friendly (more on paleo in my upcoming books)

Total Cooking Time: 2h
Prepping Time: 15m
Baking Time: 35m to 45m
Cool Time: 30m
Serving Size: 15

Ingredients

- 6 tablespoons of unsalted organic butter
- 1/2 cup coconut flour
- 1 teaspoon baking powder
- 1/2cup Dutch-process cocoa powder
- 1/4 cup cane sugar (or stevia powder)
- 1/2 teaspoon Himalayan salt
- 1 teaspoon vanilla extract
- 6 large organic eggs

Directions

1. Heat oven to 350 degrees F.
2. Prep the 8 1/2 x 4 1/2 inch loaf pan with butter.
3. Combine the coconut flour and baking powder in a strainer and sift together.
4. Place it into a mixing bowl.
5. In a saucepan heat 6 tablespoons of butter at a low heat.
6. Add cocoa powder. Stir until melted. Once smooth, transfer the melted chocolate (don't cheat! I know it's tempting especially in the winter) into a mixing bowl of large size.
7. Now add sugar or stevia, it's up to you, as well as salt, vanilla, and eggs.
8. Whisk them until they are super smooth.
9. Now you need to add in the flour mixture.
10. Whisk and then let sit for 10 minutes.
11. Place in the prep pan.
12. Bake for 35 to 45 minutes. Cool for25 minutes.
13. Remove cake from pan and let cool for another 5 minutes outside of pan.
14. Enjoy!

Tasty Coffee Cake

Like the name suggest this cake is better served with a nice cup of coffee or tea.

It's got a nice cinnamon taste and can be enjoyed on all kinds of gatherings and family occasions. Eat to your heart's content.

Total Cooking Time: 1h 10m

Prepping Time: 10m

Cooking Time: 45m – 50m

Cool Time: 10m

Serving Size: 24

Ingredients

- 2/3 cup pecans, chopped
- 2 tablespoons brown sugar or stevia
- 2 teaspoons ground cinnamon
- 1/2 cup butter (slightly melted) or coconut oil (also liquefied)
- 2 large eggs
- 1 teaspoon vanilla extract
- ¼ cup white rice flour
- ¼ tapioca flour
- ½ cup potato starch

- 1½ brown rice flour
- 1½ teaspoons xanthan gum
- 1½ teaspoons baking powder
- ¼ teaspoon baking soda
- ¼ teaspoon salt
- 1 cup cream

Directions

1. Heat oven at 350degrees F. Butter and flour 9 inch by 13 inch pan.
2. Combine the pecans, brown sugar (or stevia) and cinnamon.
3. In another mixing bowl, mix butter and eggs. Whisk energetically.
4. Add vanilla extract.
5. Combine all the **Ingredients** the white rice flour, tapioca flour, potato starch, brown rice flour, xanthan gum, baking powder, baking soda, and salt in a separate bowl.
6. Add flour mixture to creamed mixture. Slowly keep pouring batter into the pan. Top batter with pecan mixture. Spread evenly. Bake for 45-50minutes.
7. Cool for 10 minutes.
8. Serve and enjoy!

9. You can store for up to 1 week (use an air tight container). But I bet your cake won't "survive" more than 12 hours....It's not going to happen! Healthy and delicious treats have a very short lifespan.

Totally Flourless Chocolate Bundt Cake

Here comes another family friendly recipe. Kids love it! Personally, I love to serve it with some fresh fruit and nuts. I try to do my best to help my son get used to healthy snacks. I wish my family had taught me this when I was a kid...

Anyway- creating a habit of serving desserts (even though healthy and gluten-free) with fruits and nuts to snack on is an amazing nutritional tool. Just my suggestion!

Total Cooking Time: 2h 5m
Prepping Time: 35m
Baking Time: 35m to 45m
Cool Time: 45m
Serving Size: 7

Ingredients

- 1 cup of butter (make sure it's unsalted and organic, you can also use virgin coconut oil)
- 1/4 cup of cocoa powder (pick up a good brand, we want pure, organic stuff)
- 1/4cupsheavy cream
- 1 cup dark chocolate
- 5 large eggs (organic)

- ½ cup cane sugar (you can also use stevia)

Directions

1. Heat oven to 350 degrees F. Prep the 10 inch bundt pan with butter.
2. Sprinkle the pan with unsweetened cocoa powder.
3. Using a saucepan, heat the butter at a low heat.
4. Add 1/4 cup of heavy cream and stir until all of the butter is melted in the pot.
5. Add the dark chocolate and stir until totally melted. Remove from heat.

Final steps

1. Whisk the eggs, cane sugar and remaining cocoa powder.
2. Add in your chocolate.
3. Once the batter is smooth, transfer the batter to the prepped pan and bake for 35 to 45 minutes or until cake is puffed.
4. Let cool in pan for1 hour.

Body and Mind Refreshing Fruity Cake

This cake is original, nutritious and extremely energizing. Since all fruits are naturally gluten-free, I always advise my friends, readers and family to add more fruits into their diets. This delicious cake recipe may give you some ideas...Yummy yummy in my tummy!

Total Cooking Time: 1h 50m
Prepping Time: 30m
Cooking Time: 45m – 65m
Cool Time: 15m
Serving Size: 10

Ingredients

Cake Crust

- ½cup sugar (use brown, or cane or even stevia)
- ¼ cup unsalted butter
- 14 ounce sliced pineapples
- 6 maraschino cherries

Cake Batter

- 1/8white rice flour
- 1/8 tapioca flour
- Potato starch
- ¾ brown rice flour
- 1 teaspoon xanthan gum
- ½teaspoon baking powder
- ½ teaspoon salt (I use Himalayan salt)
- ½ cup butter
- ¾cup brown sugar
- ¾ cup cane sugar
- 1 large egg
- ¼ cup vanilla yogurt
- ½ cup coconut milk
- ¼ cup fresh pineapple juice
- 1 tablespoon vanilla (extract)

Directions

1. Heat oven to 350 degrees F. Separate pineapple syrup and pineapples.
2. Heat ¼ cup butter.

3. Now add the freshly melted butter to a (more or less 10 inch round) glass pie dish. Gently spread the butter around the bottom.

4. Sprinkle ½ cup sugar over it.

5. Place the pineapple on the bottom of the dish.

6. Put the cherries between pineapple slices.

7. Now take a medium bowl, to whisk together the white rice flour, tapioca flour, potato starch, brown rice flour, xanthan gum, baking powder, baking soda and salt.

8. In a separate large bowl, whisk together ½ cup of melted butter and ¾ cup sugar

9. Whisk in the egg, yogurt, coconut milk, ¼ cup of pineapple juice and then add some vanilla extract.

10. Mix thoroughly.

11. Stir in the flour mix until fully incorporated.

Final steps

1. Slowly pour your batter over the pineapple.

2. Bake for45-65 minutes.

3. Take out of oven.

4. Cool for 15-20 minutes.

5. Best served warm.

Spiced Caramel Bundt Cake

Herbs are miraculous as they have super alkalizing and anti-inflammatory properties. They also make your desserts taste sweeter. Honestly, I hardly ever use sugar (I only make an exception for my family). Thanks to herbs, we can easily do without it. Sugar is totally optional here...You can experiment and add in more powdered herbs. Cinnamon and nutmeg are my favorite. I also love them in my smoothies. Be sure to download the free eBook to learn more about healthy recipes (you can find it at the end of this book).

Total Cooking Time: 2h 43m
Prepping Time: 13m
Cooking Time: 55m
Cool Time: 1h 35m
Serving Size: 8

Ingredients

Cake

- 1 cup brown rice flour
- ¾ cup tapioca flour
- 2 teaspoons baking soda

- 1 ¼ teaspoons cinnamon (powdered)
- 1/2 teaspoon Himalayan salt
- ½ teaspoon ginger (powdered)
- ½ teaspoon nutmeg (powdered)
- 1 cup cane sugar
- ¼ cup unsalted butter
- ¼ cup organic honey
- 2 large eggs
- ¼cup olive oil
- 1 ½ cups applesauce
- ½ cup sweet white rice flour
- 1 teaspoon xanthan gum

Frosting

- ¼ cup brown sugar
- 2 tablespoons coconut cream
- 1/2 teaspoon pure vanilla (extract)

Directions

1. Heat oven to 350 degrees F. Butter 10 inch bundt pan.

2.   Combine brown rice flour, tapioca flour, sweet white rice flour, xanthan gum, baking soda, ground cinnamon, salt, ginger and nutmeg in a medium bowl. Whisk until thoroughly blended.

3.   Now take a separate bowl. Combine sugar with a quarter cup of butter and honey.

4.   Beat well until blended.

5.   Add eggs.

6.   Place them in the mixer 1 at a time so that eggs don't splash.

7.   Beat thoroughly after each mixture. Add oil.

8.   Alternate between adding flour mixture and applesauce to sugar mixture in mixing bowl.

9.   Transfer batter to prepped bundt pan.

10. Bake for 55 minutes

11. Remove from oven.

12. Cool for 15 minutes.

13. Remove from pan onto plate or tray.

Final steps

1.   Take a small saucepan to combine brown sugar and butter.

2.   Stir continuously.

3.   Cook to a boil over medium-low heat.

4. Cook for at least 1 minute. Remove from heat; add vanilla extract.

5. Take off of heat.

6. Cool for 1 minute.

7. Stir well until smooth.

8. Spoon frosting over cake.

9. Let frosting drizzle over cake.

Strawberry Super Shortcake

Here comes another delicious fruity and naturally sweet dessert recipe! Moreover, it's really quick and easy to prepare.

Total Cooking Time: 50m
Prepping Time: 30m
Cooking Time: 15m
Cool Time: 5m
Serving Size: 12

Ingredients

- ½ cup butter (be sure to get organic and unsweetened butter, otherwise you can also use coconut oil- it will make your cake taste more original)
- 1 teaspoon vanilla
- 4 organic eggs
- 1½ cup of powdered sugar
- 1cup cornstarch
- 1¼ teaspoons baking powder
- 15 strawberries, chopped
- Whipped Cream

Directions

1. To start a gluten-free baking party, first pre-heat your oven to 375 degrees F. Butter a 12-muffin pan.
2. Mix butter and sugar until creamy and fluffy.
3. Add the eggs and vanilla extract.
4. Continue to beat cream mixture.
5. In a small bowl mix the cornstarch and baking powder together.
6. Slowly add the creamed mixture.
7. Mix until well blended.
8. Fill half of the greased muffin tins with batter.
9. Bake for 15 minutes (so that a toothpick that is inserted into the center and comes out clean)
10. Remove from the pan while warm.
11. Cool for 5 minutes.
12. Serve with strawberries and some whipped cream on top
13. Enjoy! We do!

Snickerdoodle

Total Cooking Time: 40m
Prepping Time: 20m
Cooking Time: 10m
Cool Time: 10m
Serving Size: 48

Ingredients

- 1 cup sugar
- ½ cup butter, softened
- 1cuprice flour
- 1/3 cup potato starch
- 1/6 cup tapioca flour
- 1 teaspoon xanthan gum
- 1 large egg
- 1 teaspoon cream of tartar
- ½ cup vanilla (extract)
- Pinch of salt
- 2teaspoon cinnamon (powdered)

Directions

1. To start our healthy baking party, pre-heat your oven to 400 degrees Fahrenheit.
2. Combine ¾ cup sugar and butter in bowl.
3. Beat energetically.
4. Add egg, cream of tartar, vanilla extract, salt, rice flour, potato starch, tapioca flour, and xanthan gum.
5. In a small bowl, combine 3 tablespoons of sugar with half a teaspoon of cinnamon.
6. Scoop dough into tablespoons.
7. Roll into balls. Rollin cinnamon – sugar mixture.
8. Place on ungreased cookie sheet. Bake for 8-10 minutes.
9. Let cool down for 10 minutes.

Spiced Caramel Bundt Cake

Here comes another spicy-tasting recipe. Ginger is a powerful antioxidant, has anti-inflammatory properties and will make your desserts taste great! Would I want to go back to packaged and processed cakes? No, never. I prefer to make my own!

Total Cooking Time: 2h 43m
Prepping Time: 13m
Cooking Time: 55m
Cool Time: 1h 35m
Serving Size: 8

Ingredients

Cake

- 1 cup brown rice flour
- ¾ cup tapioca flour
- ½ cup sweet white rice flour
- 1 teaspoon xanthan gum
- 2 teaspoons baking soda
- 1¼ teaspoons ground cinnamon
- 1 teaspoon salt
- ½ teaspoon ground ginger

- ½ teaspoon ground nutmeg
- 1 cup cane sugar
- ¼ cup unsalted butter
- ¼ cup honey
- 2 large eggs
- ¼ cup coconut oil
- 1 ½ cups applesauce

Frosting

- ¼ cup brown sugar
- 3 tablespoons half and half
- 2 tablespoons unsalted butter
- 1/2 teaspoon vanilla (extract)
- 3/4 cup sugar (cane, or stevia, you can also use powdered sugar, or just do without it. I always say that sugar is optional)

Directions

1. Heat oven to 350 degrees F. Butter 10-inch bundt pan.
2. Combine brown rice flour, tapioca flour, sweet white rice flour, xanthan gum, baking soda, ground cinnamon, salt, ginger and nutmeg in a medium bowl.

3. Whisk until thoroughly blended.

4. In a separate bowl, combine sugar, 1/4 cup of butter and honey.

5. Beat with at medium speed until well blended.

6. Add eggs. Place them in the mixer 1 at a time so that eggs don't splash. Beat thoroughly after each mixture.

7. Add oil. Alternate between adding flour mixture and applesauce to sugar mixture in mixing bowl.

8. Transfer batter to prepped bundt pan.

9. Bake for 55 minutes.

10. Remove from oven.

11. Cool for 15 minutes. Remove from pan onto plate or tray.

Final steps

1. In a small saucepan, combine brown sugar, half and half and 2 tablespoons of butter.

2. Stir continuously.

3. Cook to a boil over medium-low heat.

4. Cook for at least 1 minute.

5. Remove from heat; add vanilla extract.

6. Stir in vanilla extract.

7. Take off of heat.

8. Cool for 1 minute; add powdered sugar.

9. Stir with a whisk until smooth.

10. Spoon frosting over cake.

11. Let frosting drizzle over cake.

Sugar Cookies

Total Cooking Time: 4h 7m
Prepping Time: 45m
Cooking Time: 12m
Cool Time: 3h 10m
Serving Size: 36

Ingredients

- ½ cup of butter (make sure it's unsalted organic, as an alternative you can also use coconut oil)
- 1/2 cup sugar (cane, brown or stevia- choose what you prefer)
- 1 organic egg
- 1 tsp vanilla extract
- 1/3 cup white rice flour
- 1/3 cup tapioca flour
- 2/3 cup potato starch
- 1 3/4 brown rice flour
- 2 tsp baking powder
- 1/4 tsp Himalayan salt
- 1/3 cup milk

Directions

1. First mix sugar and butter in a mixing bowl. Then beat until very creamy.
2. Add egg and the vanilla extract.
3. Mix until all ingredients are combined thoroughly.
4. In another bowl, combine the white rice flour, tapioca flour, potato starch, brown rice flour, baking powder and salt.
5. Whisk for 3 minutes. Transfer flour mix into mixing bowl alternate between adding flour mix and milk until thick dough forms.
6. Add to a mixing bowl. Cover.
7. Place in a fridge for at least 3 hours.

Final steps

1. Heat oven to 375 degrees Fahrenheit.
2. Prep baking sheet with parchment paper.
3. Scoop dough with teaspoon.
4. Place dough on baking sheet.
5. Place 2inches apart on pan to allow for spreading.
6. Bake for 10-12 minutes or until slightly golden brown around the edges.

7.   Cool on pan for 5 minutes.

Almond Macaroons

Total Cooking Time: 30m

Prepping Time: 20m

Baking Time: 10m

Cool Time: 10m

Serving Size: 16

Ingredients

- 1 cup chopped almonds
- 14 whole almonds
- 2/3 cup cane sugar
- 1 large egg white
- 1/4 teaspoon almond extract
- 1/8 salt
- Powdered sugar (use for dusting)

Directions

1. To start the healthy gluten-free baking party, pre-heat oven to 350 degrees F.
2. Prep a baking sheet with butter.
3. Blend the chopped almonds and add in the cane sugar until finely ground.

4. Add egg white, almond extract and salt.

5. Pulse until completely combined. Roll mixture into 14 balls.

6. Arrange 2 inches apart on baking sheet.

7. Flatten Balls slightly.

8. Sprinkle powdered sugar on onto each cookie.

9. Push almond into each cookie.

10. Bake macaroons in the oven for 10 minutes.

11. Let cool for 10 minutes and serve.

12. Keep in airtight container for 1 week at room temperature.

13. Enjoy!

Caramel Apple Cookies

Apple cookies are excellent natural, home-made snacks. Kids love it and always look forward to taking some with them for their school excursions and lunches. My husband always takes some with him to the gym. If you need quick energy they can really sort you out.

Total Cooking Time: 50m
Prepping Time: 35m
Cooking Time: 15m
Cool Time: 5m
Serving Size: 24

Ingredients

Cookie

- ½ cup of unsalted butter, slightly melted
- ½ cup sugar of your choice
- 1 large organic egg
- 2 tablespoons coconut milk or almond milk
- ¾teaspoon vanilla extract
- 1/8 cup white rice flour
- 1/8 cup tapioca flour

- ¼ cup potato starch
- ¾ cup brown rice flour
- ¾ teaspoon baking soda
- ¼ teaspoon salt
- 1 ½ cups gluten-free rolled oats
- 2 apples, chopped and peeled

Caramel

- 1 cup sugar of your choice
- 6 tablespoons butter
- ½ cup cream (I suggest coconut cream as it is natural)
- 1 teaspoon Himalayan salt

Directions

1. To get the party rolling, first pre-heat your oven to 325 degrees F.
2. Mix the butter and sugar until creamy and fluffy.
3. Add egg, milk, and vanilla.
4. Continue to mix until fluffy.
5. In a separate mixing bowl, combine white rice flour, tapioca flour, potato starch and brown rice flour.
6. Mix until ingredients are thoroughly combined.
7. Add baking soda, and salt stir with a whisk.

8. Stir in oats.

9. Add oat and flour mixture to cream mixture.

10. Beat until blended. Stir in apples and fold.

11. Place parchment paper on cookie sheets.

12. Scoop dough with 1 ½ tablespoon. Place cookies 2 inches apart onto baking sheet. Bake for about 15 minutes.

13. Transfer cookies to wire racks let cool completely.

Final steps

1. Heat cane sugar.

2. Stir with heat safe spatula until the sugar is melted into a thick brown liquid. Be careful not to let sugar burn in pan.

3. When melted, add the butter on low heat.

4. Stir the butter so that it melts

5. Now slowly add in half cup of cream.

6. Stir energetically.

7. Boil for 30 seconds.

8. Remove from heat.

9. Then add in 1 teaspoon of salt.

10. Allow to cool down for 5 minutes.

11. Drizzle caramel over cookies.

12. Let stand until caramel is completely set.

13. Enjoy!

Magic Cherry Fresh Tart

This recipe calls for cherries, but you could also use strawberries, blueberries or other fruit. I love to serve this tart with some home-made peanut butter or marmalade. So yummy!

Total Cooking Time: 1h 30m
Prepping Time: 35m
Cooking Time: 30m
Cool Time: 25m
Serving Size: 24

Ingredients

Cherry Filling

- 1 cup dark cherries, pitted
- 2 tablespoons lemon juice
- ½ cup cane sugar

Cookie Tarts:

- 1/8 cup white rice flour
- 1/8 tapioca flour

- ¼ potato starch
- ¾ brown rice flour
- 1 teaspoon baking powder
- 1/8 teaspoon Himalayan salt
- ½ cup butter, softened
- ½ cup cane sugar
- 1½ teaspoon vanilla (extracted)

Directions

1. Heat oven to 350 degrees F.
2. In a medium saucepan combine pitted cherries, lemon juice and sugar.
3. Cook over medium-low heat.
4. Stir frequently with fork.
5. Use fork to mash cherries.
6. Cook for 15 minutes or until the mixture turns to a cherry jam.
7. Set aside to let it cool.
8. Grease a mini muffin pan with some butter.
9. In a medium bowl add white rice flour, tapioca flour, potato starch, brown rice flour, baking powder, and salt.
10. Use a whisk to stir ingredients. Set aside.
11. Combine butter and vanilla extract (use a medium-sized mixing bowl)

12. Beat until fluffy.

13. Add the sugar and continue to beat for a few minutes.

14. Add all the dry ingredients and mix energetically.

Final steps

1. Scoop batter in tablespoons and place the tart cookie dough into mini muffin cups.

2. Gently press the dough with the tablespoon, up the sides of the muffin cups leaving an indentation in the middle of the cookie.

3. Check that the bottom is thick enough to hold cherry filling. Add a rounded ½ teaspoon of jam in the center of each tart. Leave space for tart filling to expand.

4. Bake for 9-15 minutes or until a light golden brown is seen on the edges of the tarts.

5. Remove tarts from muffin pan and place on tray.

6. Cool the tarts on surface for 15minutes then place the tarts into the freezer for 10 minutes.

7. Serve and enjoy!

Chocolate Almond Meringues

Almond flour is another gluten-free flour and it is especially loved by Paleo diet fans.

Total Cooking Time: 1h 50m

Prepping Time: 30m

Cooking Time: 1h 10m

Cool Time: 10

Serving Size: 10

Ingredients

- 1/ cup stevia powder
- 1/2 cup almond flour
- 1 pinch of Himalayan salt
- 1/4 cup sugar (cane, brown or stevia)
- 1/2 tsp natural vanilla extract
- 1/3 cup dark chocolate, chopped
- 1/4 cup cocoa
- 4 large egg whites

Directions

1. Heat oven to 300 degrees Fahrenheit.

2. Combine the stevia, almond flour and cocoa in a mixing bowl.

3. Stir with a whisk.

4. In a large bowl mix egg whites on medium speed.

5. Add sugar.

6. Then add vanilla extract, and then use a spatula to fold in flour mix and chopped chocolate.

7. Scoop batter with tablespoon onto a baking sheet with parched paper sheet on top.

8. Bake for 10 minutes.

9. Reduce oven temperature to 200 degrees and bake for 1 hour more.

10. Cool for 10 minutes.

11. Serve and enjoy!

12. Store in an air tight container.

Peanut Butter Cookies

Total Cooking Time: 35m

Prepping Time: 20m

Baking Time: 6m to 12m

Cool Time: 3m

Serving Size: 12

Ingredients

- 1 cup almond flour (blanched)
- 1/2 teaspoon Himalayan salt
- 1/4 teaspoon baking soda
- 1/2cupcreamy peanut butter
- 1/4 cup raw organic honey
- 2 tablespoon palm shortening
- 1teaspoon vanilla extract

Directions

1. Heat oven to 350 degrees F.
2. Prep a baking sheet with butter.
3. In a small bowl combine almond flour with Himalayan salt and baking soda.

4. Mix together peanut butter, honey, shortening and vanilla extract. (use a medium-sized bowl)

5. Add flour mixture.

6. Scoop dough into a tablespoon onto prepped baking sheet.

7. Use a fork to flatten in a crisscross pattern. Bake for 6 to 12 minutes until golden around the edges.

8. Cool for 3 minutes.

9. Serve and store in airtight container for 3 days.

Caramel Apples

Total Cooking Time: 2h 15m

Prepping Time: 1h

Cooking Time: 15m

Cool Time: 1h

Serving Size: 10

Ingredients

- 10 wooden sticks
- 10 small apples
- 2 cups brown sugar
- ½ cup corn syrup
- ½cup water
- 2 cups half and half
- 2 teaspoons vanilla extract
- ¼ teaspoon salt

Directions

1. Insert wooden sticks into the apples.
2. Place apples in the refrigerator and set aside.
3. Mix sugar, corn syrup and water.
4. Stir to prevent sugar from bubbling.

5. Wait for mixture to boil.

6. Add half and half, vanilla extract and salt.

7. Stir as you add ingredients.

8. Now, reduce heat to low.

9. Boil for 15 minutes.

10. Take pot off of heat.

11. Massage apples in caramel.

12. Then, place on baking sheet (lined with wax paper)

Caramelized Pineapple with Vanilla Ice Cream

This is a simple and refreshing, quick summer recipe.

You can also add in some powdered herbs like cinnamon and nutmeg.

Enjoy!

Total Cooking Time: 15m

Prepping Time: 10m

Serving Size: 4

Ingredients

- 4 tablespoons of butter (unsalted, organic)
- 1/2 cup sugar of your choice
- 1 pineapple cut into half moons
- 4 scoops of natural vanilla ice cream

Directions

1. Melt butter in a skillet.
2. Add sugar and cook.
3. Stir for 1 minute or until butter is melted and caramelized.
4. Add pineapple and cook.

5. Stir in pan so that pineapple is tender.

6. Let it cool for about 20 minutes

7. Serve pineapple with some ice cream and drizzle with caramel pineapple sauce.

Chocolate Mousse

Total Cooking Time: 4h 30m

Prepping Time: 30m

Cool Time: 3h to 4h

Serving Size: 5

Ingredients

- 1 cup cold whip

Cream

- 1/2 cup cane sugar
- 1/4 cup water
- 3/4 cup of milk chocolate
- 2 large organic eggs
- 1/2 teaspoon of instant coffee

Directions

1. Add water to a medium sauce pan.
2. Let boil.
3. Add sugar.
4. Mix until sugar is 100% dissolved.

5. Reduce heat to low and add chocolate until completely melted.

6. Stir until smooth.

Final steps

1. Combine instant coffee and eggs into a food processor.

2. Pulse until eggs are blended.

3. Slowly add chocolate mixture into bowl as processor is still running.

4. Process until smooth.

5. Add whip cream.

6. Once it is evenly distributed, place mousse into container.

7. Place plastic wrap over container.

8. Refrigerate for 3 to 4 hours.

9. Stir before serving.

10. Serve immediately.

Yummy Fudge

Total Cooking Time: 1h 5m

Prepping Time: 5m

Cool Time: 2h

Serving Size: 36

Ingredients

- 4 cups powdered sugar
- 1/2 cup cocoa (unsweetened)
- 1/4salt
- 1/4 cup milk
- 1tablespoon vanilla
- 1/2 cup butter

Directions

1. In a mixing bowl stir together sugar, cocoa, salt, milk and vanilla until slightly blended.
2. Transfer into casserole dish.
3. Place butter over fudge.
4. Microwave for two minutes.
5. Stir until smooth.
6. Pour into a butter prepped 8-inch square dish.

7. Chill in refrigerator for 1 hour.

Cherry Rice Pudding

Total Cooking Time: 1h 50m

Prepping Time: 30m

Cooking Time: 45m – 65m

Cool Time: 15m

Serving Size: 10

Ingredients

Cake Crust

- ½ cup brown sugar
- ¼ cup unsalted butter
- 14 ounce sliced pineapples
- 6 maraschino cherries

Cake Batter

- 1/8 white rice flour
- 1/8 tapioca flour
- ¼ potato starch
- ¾ brown rice flour
- 1 teaspoon xanthan gum

- ½ teaspoon baking powder
- ½teaspoon salt
- ½ cup butter
- ¾ cup brown sugar
- ¾ cup cane sugar
- 1 large egg
- ¼ cup vanilla yogurt
- ½ cup milk
- ¼ cup pineapple juice
- 1 tablespoon vanilla (extract)

Directions

1. Heat oven to 350 degrees F. Separate pineapple syrup and pineapples.
2. Heat ¼ cup butter.
3. Add it to a 9 inch round glass pie dish and spread it around the bottom.
4. Sprinkle over some sugar.
5. Place pineapple slices on the bottom of the dish and put the cherries in the open spaces between pineapple slices inside the holes.

6. In a medium bowl, combine and whisk the white rice flour, tapioca flour, potato starch, brown rice flour, xanthan gum, baking powder, baking soda and salt.

7. In a separate bowl, whisk ½ cup of melted butter, ¾ cup brown sugar and cane sugar use whisk thoroughly.

8. Whisk in the egg, yogurt, milk, ¼ cup of pineapple juice and vanilla extract. Mix thoroughly.

9. Stir in the flour mix until fully incorporated.

Final steps

1. Spread the batter over the pineapple.

2. Bake for 45-65 minutes.

3. Take out of oven.

4. Cool cake in the dish for 15-20 minutes.

5. Best served warm.

6. Enjoy and eat to your heart's content!

Strawberry and Peach Parfait

Total Cooking Time: 10m

Prepping Time: 10m

Serving Size: 4

Ingredients

- 1 cup peach (chopped)
- 2 cup strawberries
- 2 cup pure quinoa
- 4 small containers of strawberry yogurt

Directions

1. Combine peaches and strawberries in a salad bowl.
2. Transfer a spoon full of fruit into four separate cups or bowls.
3. Add a spoonful of yogurt onto fruit.
4. Layer on quinoa.
5. Add spoon of fruit.
6. Layer on yogurt and then quinoa.
7. Repeat until satisfied with portion or ingredients are gone.
8. Enjoy!

Vanilla Chocolate Pudding Pops

Total Cooking Time: 2h 30m

Prepping Time: 20m

Cool Time: 2h

Freezing Time: 10

Serving Size: 6

Ingredients

- 2/3 cup cane sugar
- 4tablespoons cornstarch
- 1/2 teaspoon Himalayan salt
- 4 cups coconut milk
- 6large egg yolks
- 6 tablespoons butter (unsalted, organic)
- 4 teaspoons vanilla extract
- 6 ounces of bittersweet chocolate

Directions

1. Prep cooking area by placing two strainers over two separate mixing bowls.
2. Now combine the cane sugar with Himalayan salt and cornstarch. Whisk in a large saucepan.

3. Drizzle 1/2 of milk into it.

4. Whisk until smooth. Add egg yolks slowly while whisking. Add remaining milk.

5. Separate ingredients into two saucepans. Place saucepans over medium heat.

6. Cook.

7. In first saucepan add chocolate and whisk until pudding is smooth. In second saucepan whisk for 5 minutes.

8. As they both start to bubble, reduce heat to medium low. Stir both with separate spatulas. Do not let bottom or sides burn.

9. After 3 to 5 minutes of stirring remove from heat, divide butter and vanilla extract into two separate bowls.

10. Stir in butter mixtures into each saucepan. Stir until both are melted.

11. Strain the pudding.

12. Transfer into two containers.

13. Cover container with plastic wrap. Chill in fridge for 2 hours.

14. Remove from fridge and transfer into 4 oz paper cups

15. Freeze for 10 minutes combine vanilla and chocolate pudding.

16. Insert wooden sticks. Freeze for 3 hours. Serve immediately.

17. Enjoy!

Vanilla Pudding

Total Cooking Time: 2h 20m

Prepping Time: 20m

Cool Time: 2h

Serving Size: 6

Ingredients

- 1/3 cup cane sugar
- 2 tablespoons cornstarch
- 1/4 teaspoon Himalayan salt
- 2 Coconut milk
- 3 egg yolks
- 3 tablespoons butter (organic, unsalted)
- 2 teaspoons vanilla (extract)

Directions

1. Prep cooking area by placing strainer over a mixing bowl.
2. Take a medium-sized saucepan. Combine the sugar, cornstarch, and salt. Whisk well.
3. Drizzle 1/4 of milk into saucepan and whisk until smooth.
4. Add egg yolks slowly while whisking.
5. Add remaining milk.

Final steps

1. Place saucepan over medium heat and cook.

2. Whisk until pudding is thick for 5 minutes.

3. When bubbling, reduce heat to low. Stir with spatula. Do not let bottom or sides burn.

4. After 3 to 5 minutes of stirring remove from heat and stir in butter.

5. Add vanilla extract until both butter and extract are melted.

6. Pour the pudding through the strainer.

7. Place into a container.

8. Cover container with plastic wrap.

9. Chill in fridge for a couple of hours

10. Serve, enjoy and eat to your heart's content.

Nutritious Paradise Ambrosia

This recipe will provide you with many vital nutrients. Say thanks to fruits and nuts! It's also dairy-free (say thanks to coconut cream that is healthy and nutritious). One more thing- as you already know herbs have anti-inflammatory properties and are a great component of healthy gluten-free desserts. Eat to your heart's content!

Total Cooking Time: 1h 15m
Prepping Time: 30m
Cool Time: 30m – 45m
Serving Size: 4

Ingredients

- Thick Coconut Cream
- 1tablespoon of sugar or stevia
- ½cup walnuts, chopped
- 1 cup pecans, chopped
- 1 can fruit cocktail
- 1 can pineapple chunks
- 1 cup Clementine oranges, slices
- 3 cups miniature marshmallows

- 1 jar maraschino cherries
- 1teaspoon nutmeg (powdered)
- 1 teaspoon cinnamon (powdered)
- 1 cup coconut, grated

Directions

1. Mix the coconut cream, coconut, chopped nuts, fruit cocktail, pineapple, clementine oranges, marshmallows, cherries, nutmeg and cinnamon (use a salad bowl)
2. Mix together well and refrigerate for 30 to 45 minutes.
3. Serve and enjoy!

Amazing Butterscotch Pudding with Toffee

Total Cooking Time: 2h 10m

Prepping Time: 1h

Cooking Time: 10m

Cool Time: 1h

Serving Size: 6

Ingredients

- 1 ½ cup brown sugar
- ¼ cup cornstarch (pure, gluten-free)
- ½ teaspoon salt
- 3 cups coconut milk
- 4 large eggs yolks
- 2 tablespoons butter
- Skor Bar, grated

Directions

1. First, mix the brown sugar, cornstarch, and salt.
2. In a separate bowl, whisk together the milk and egg yolks.

3. Once well blended, pour egg mixture into the pan with the brown sugar mixture and stir to combine.

4. Place pudding mixture in a large saucepan on medium heat.

5. Stir mixture for 10 minutes or until it begins to bubble.

6. Stir in butter after the pudding mixture becomes thickened. Let butter melt completely. Remove the saucepan from heat and let chill for 1 hour or more.

7. Place plastic wrap over container so that pudding doesn't develop skin on the top.

8. After pudding has chilled for 1-hour grate skor bar over the top of pudding.

9. Serve immediately.

10. Refrigerate for up to 2 days.

11. Enjoy!

Super Sweet Banana Pudding

Sugar is totally optional in this recipe. Personally, I find bananas sweet enough!

This pudding will keep up to 2 days (if stored in a fridge).

Enjoy!

Total Cooking Time: 1h 35m

Prepping Time: 1h

Cooking Time: 25m

Cool Time: 10m (overnight)

Serving Size: 10

Ingredients

Cookie

- ¾ cup sugar (optional)
- ½ cup butter, softened
- 1 large Egg
- 1/2 teaspoon vanilla extract
- 1/8 cup white rice flour
- 1/8 cup tapioca flour
- ¼ cup potato starch
- ¾ cup brown rice flour

- 1/2 teaspoon baking soda

Pudding

- 1/3 cup cane sugar (optional)
- 2 tablespoons cornstarch
- 1/4 teaspoon salt
- 2 cups coconut milk
- 3 large egg yolks
- 3 tablespoons butter (make sure it's unsalted)
- 2 teaspoons vanilla (extracted)
- 4 Bananas, sliced
- Whipped Cream or coconut cream

Directions

1. To make the magic, heat oven to 400 degrees F.
2. Combine sugar, butter, egg and vanilla in a medium bowl.
3. Beat well.
4. Add white rice flour, tapioca flour, potato starch, brown rice flour to bowl.
5. Blend in baking soda.
6. Make sure it's all well mixed.
7. Shape dough into ½ inch balls.

8. Place each cookie 1 inch apart onto ungreased cookie sheets. Flatten.

9. Bake 10-15 minutes.

10. Take cookies off of cookie sheet and let cool for 15 minutes.

11. Place in airtight container and let them sit overnight in room temperature environment.

12. Prep cooking area by placing strainer over a mixing bowl.

13. Combine the sugar and cornstarch.

14. Add salt and whisk well.

15. Drizzle 1/4 of milk into saucepan and whisk until smooth. Add egg yolks slowly while whisking.

16. Add remaining milk.

Final steps

1. Place saucepan over medium heat and cook.

2. Whisk until pudding is thick for 5 minutes.

3. As it starts to bubble, reduce heat to medium low.

4. Stir with spatula.

5. Do not let bottom or sides burn.

6. After 3 to 5 minutes of stirring remove from heat and stir in butter.

7. Add vanilla extract until both butter and extract are melted.

8. Pour the pudding through the strainer.

9. Cover and chill in fridge overnight.

The following day place cookies at the bottom of a glass pie dish. Top with layer of banana slices and pudding. Repeat layering process. Cover with whipped cream. Crush the remaining cookies and place them in a container. Refrigerate for 3 hours. Serve individual portions with cookie crumbs sprinkled on top for a mild crunch.

Enjoy!

Super Tasty Cheesecake Bars

This is my favorite comfort dessert. What can beat cheesecake?

Total Cooking Time: 1h 30m

Prepping Time: 40m (-12m)

Cooking Time: 42m

Cool Time: 20m

Serving Size: 12

Ingredients

Crust

- 1/4 cup organic butter
- 1/4 cup brown sugar
- 1/2 cup walnuts (chopped)
- 1cup almond flour

Filling

- 1/4 cup cane sugar
- 8ounces organic cream cheese
- 1 tablespoon lemon juice

- 2 tablespoons coconut milk
- 1 organic egg
- 1/2 teaspoon vanilla extract

Directions

1. Heat oven to 350 degrees F.
2. Combine sugar and butter.
3. Add almond flour and chopped nuts and stir until crumbly.
4. Press mixture into an 8-inch square pan and bake for 12 minutes.
5. Let cool and set aside.
6. Combine white sugar and cream cheese in a mixing bowl.
7. Beat until smooth.
8. Stir in egg, milk, lemon juice and vanilla extract. Mix until smooth.
9. Finally, spread all the filling over your crust.
10. Then, bake for half an hour.
11. Cool in refrigerate for 20 minutes.
12. Cut into squares and serve.

Nice'n'Fresh Lemon Bars

Total Cooking Time: 1h 5m

Prepping Time: 15m

Cooking Time: 40m

Cool Time: 10m

Serving Size: 12

Ingredients

- 1/2 cup butter, softened (you can also use coconut oil
- 2 cups almond flour
- 4large eggs
- 2 cup cane sugar
- 2 lemons juiced

Directions

1. Heat oven to 350 degrees F.
2. Mix butter, flour and ½ cup of sugar (use a medium size bowl)
3. Mix until well combined.
4. Place aluminum foil over an 8-inch square pan.
5. Press flour combination into the bottom of the pan.
6. Then bake for 15 to 20 minutes until golden.

Final steps

1. In another bowl, combine another ½ cup of sugar and ¼ cup of flour.
2. Whisk in each egg individually and add lemon juice.
3. Mix until super smooth.
4. Pour over the baked crust.
5. Bake for 20 minutes in oven.
6. Remove immediately and let cool for 10 minutes.
7. Serve when firm.
8. Cut into squares.

Original Pecan Pie

Total Cooking Time: 3h 35m

Prepping Time: 45m

Cooking Time: 40m - 45m

Cool Time: 45m

Serving Size: 8

Ingredients

Dough:

- 1/8 cup white rice flour
- 1/8 cup tapioca flour
- ¼ cup potato starch
- ¾cup of brown rice flour
- 2tablespoons sweet rice flour
- 1 ½ teaspoons cane sugar
- Pinch of Himalayan salt
- 6 tablespoons of unsalted butter,
- 1large egg
- lemon juice, 1 tablespoon

Filling:

- 5 tablespoons unsalted butter
- 1 cup brown sugar
- ¾ cup corn syrup
- ½teaspoon fine salt
- 2 cups pecans (chopped)
- 2 tablespoons of bourbon
- 2 teaspoons vanilla (extracted)
- 3 eggs

Directions

1. Take a large bowl.
2. Mix the white rice flour, tapioca flour, potato starch, brown rice flour, sweet rice flour, 1 ½ cup of sugar and 1/8 teaspoon of salt.
3. Stir until thoroughly blended. Take butter and place on top of flour mixture.
4. Work the butter into the flour mixture.
5. Form a coarse meal.
6. Push a ½ cup measuring cup into the center of the coarse meal.
7. Make sure to leave a dent in the middle of dough.

8. Break egg into the well. Add the lemon juice.

9. Use a fork and stir well.

10. Knead the flour into the egg to form soft dough.

11. Shape into a pie disk and chill in the freezer for 60 minutes.

12. Heat oven at 400 degrees F.

13. Place flour on a flat cooking surface.

14. Use roller to flatten pie dough.

15. Press the pie pastry into the prepped pie pan.

16. Bake for 12 to 15 minutes.

17. Take out of oven and let cool for 15 minutes.

18. Mix the butter, salt, brown sugar, corn syrup. Whisk well in a saucepan.

19. Boil and stir constantly. (use medium heat)

20. Boil for 1 minute.

21. Now, remove from heat. Add in vanilla, nuts and bourbon.

22. Set aside for a few minutes.

23. In a small bowl, whisk 3 eggs until fully beaten.

24. Slowly whisk the beaten eggs into the filling.

25. When filling and egg is completely incorporated place the pie crust on a sheet pan to prevent bottom of crust from burning.

26. Transfer the filling into the crust.

Final steps

1. Bakefor40 to 45 minutes.
2. Cool on a rack for 15 minutes to let pecan filling set.
3. Add a side of vanilla ice cream for a complimenting taste or serve with fresh fruits or marmalade of your choice.

Natural Apple Crisp

Total Cooking Time: 60 mins
Cooking Time: 30 mins
Cool Time: 30 mins
Serving Size: 6

Ingredients

Filling

- 4 large apples, chopped
- 2 teaspoons lemon juice
- 1/4 cup cane sugar
- 1/3 cup pure maple syrup
- 1teaspoon vanilla extract
- 1 ½ tablespoon cornstarch
- 1teaspoon ground cinnamon

Topping

- 1/3cup packed brown sugar
- ¾ cup quinoa
- ½ almond flour
- ½ ground cinnamon

- Pinch of Himalayan salt
- 1/3 cup unsalted butter, melted (you can also use coconut oil)

Directions

1. Heat oven to 350 degrees Fahrenheit.
2. In a large bowl, mix the vanilla extract, cornstarch and cinnamon, lemon juice, cane sugar and maple syrup together.
3. Whisk until all ingredients are thoroughly combined. Add apples. Stir well.
4. Spoon apples into a 9 inch pie dish. Set aside.
5. Combine brown sugar, quinoa, and almond flour together. Whisk them for 1 minute.
6. Add cinnamon and salt.
7. Stir butter until well combined.
8. Sprinkle topping mixture over apples.
9. Bake for half an hour.
10. Cool for half an hour.
11. Serve with some fresh fruit.
12. Store leftovers in refrigerator for less than one week.

Super Cream Pie

Total Cooking Time: 7h 35m

Prepping Time: 1h 10m

Cooking Time: 25m

Cool Time: 6h 10m (overnight)

Serving Size: 10

Ingredients

Filling

- ⅓ cup coconut milk
- 2 cups heavy cream (you can also use coconut cream)
- 2 ½ tablespoons cornstarch
- 1 large egg yolk
- 1/3 cup sugar (cane or stevia)
- Pinch of Himalayan salt
- 1tablespoon vanilla extract

Crust

- ¼ cup sweet white rice flour
- 1/8 cup tapioca flour
- ¼ cup potato starch

- ¾ cup brown rice flour
- 1 teaspoon sugar (cane, brown or stevia)
- Pinch of Himalayan salt
- 6 tablespoons unsalted butter
- 1 large egg
- 1 tablespoon lemon juice
- Whipped cream
- Pinch of ground cinnamon (optional)

Directions

1. Mix the milk and 1-1/3 cup of the heavy cream.
2. Add the cornstarch in the cream mixture.
3. Whisk in the egg yolk.
4. Set aside.
5. In a large saucepan, mix in 1/3 cup of sugar and 1/8 teaspoon of salt.
6. Add remaining 2/3 heavy cream into saucepan.
7. Place saucepan at medium heat.
8. Bring the mixture to a simmer and remove from heat.
9. Whisk half of the sugar mixture into the medium bowl with the cream mixture and stir until combination is well blended.
10. Stir the contents of the bowl into the large saucepan.

11. Return to medium heat and stir often for five minutes or until mixture thickens.

12. Remove from heat.

13. Add in 1 teaspoon vanilla extract.

14. Strain into a bowl.

15. Cover. Let it chill for 3 hours.

16. Heat oven at 400 degrees F. Butter pie pan.

17. In a large bowl, combine the white rice flour, tapioca flour, potato starch, brown rice flour, sweet rice flour, 1 ½ cup of sugar and 1/8 teaspoon of salt. Stir until thoroughly blended.

18. Take butter and place on top of flour mixture.

19. Work the butter into the flour mixture to form a coarse meal. Make a well in the coarse meal by pushing a ½ cup measuring cup into the center of the coarse meal.

20. Make sure to leave a dent in the middle of dough. Break egg into the well. Add the lemon juice. Knead the flour into the egg to form soft dough. Make sure dough is well blended.

21. Shape into a pie disk then chill in the fridge. (40 mins)

Final steps

1. Place flour on a flat cooking surface.

2. Use roller to flatten pie dough.

3. Press the pie pastry into the prepped pie pan.

4. Bake until golden brown for 12 to 15 minutes.

5. Take out of oven and let cool for 15 minutes.

6. Take your chilled filling (the one you placed in fridge in the previous step)

7. Pour it into the crust.

8. Cover.

9. Place in a fridge for3 hours or overnight for perfect consistency.

10. Top pie with some cream and cinnamon.

11. Serve.

12. Store in refrigerator for up to 1 week.

So Good Peach Cobbler

Total Cooking Time: 1h 10m

Prepping Time: 10m

Cooking Time: 35m

Cool Time: 15m

Serving Size: 8

Ingredients

Filling

- (2) 29 oz cans of sliced peaches in syrup
- 1 ¼ cup of peach syrup
- 1 tablespoon ground cinnamon
- ¼ teaspoon ground nutmeg
- 1 tablespoon cornstarch

Crust

- 1.5 cup cane sugar
- 1/8 cup white flour rice
- 1/8 cup tapioca flour
- ¼ potato starch
- 1 cup brown rice flour

- 1 ¾ teaspoon gluten free baking powder
- ½ teaspoon salt
- 1 large egg
- 6 tablespoons butter (organic, unsalted) or: use coconut oil
- 2 tablespoons milk
- ½ teaspoon vanilla extract

Directions

1. Heat oven to 350 degrees F. Open can of peaches.
2. Pour 1 cup of syrup into a bowl; pour another ¼ cup of syrup into a cup. Set aside both.
3. Drain the rest of the peaches into a strainer.
4. Place drained peaches in mixing bowl.
5. Combine cinnamon, nutmeg and cornstarch into the bowl with the syrup and blend ingredients together.
6. Add peaches and stir well.
7. Place peach mixture into an 11 inch by 7 inch Pyrex dish. Set aside.
8. In a separate mixing bowl, combine white flour rice, tapioca flour, potato starch, brown rice flour, baking powder and salt.
9. Whisk energetically.

10. Add the cup of peach syrup, egg, butter, milk and vanilla extract.

11. Beat well.

12. Sprinkle surface with flour.

13. Place batter over surface.

14. Use a roller to flatten batter.

15. Place batter over peaches in Pyrex.

16. Brush batter with melted butter.

17. In a small bowl, combine ¼ cup of cinnamon and 2 teaspoons of sugar.

18. Once thoroughly, blended sprinkle ground cinnamon mix over batter.

19. Bake for 40 minutes until batter is golden brown.

20. Cool for 25 minutes so that sauce can thicken inside the cobbler.

21. Serve.

Peanut Butter Pie

Total Cooking Time: 3h 35m

Prepping Time: 20m

Cooking Time: 1h 15m

Cool Time: 2h

Serving Size: 8

Ingredients

Dough:

- 1/8 cup white rice flour
- 1/8 cup tapioca flour
- ¼ cup potato starch
- ¾ cup brown rice flour
- 2 tablespoons sweet rice flour
- 1 ½ teaspoon sugar
- 1/8 teaspoon salt
- 6 tablespoons unsalted butter
- 1largeegg
- 1 tablespoon lemon juice

Filling:

- 8-ounce cream cheese
- ½ cup creamy peanut butter
- ½ cup powdered sugar
- Whipped Cream

Directions

1. In a large bowl, combine the white rice flour, tapioca flour, potato starch, brown rice flour, sweet rice flour, 1 ½ cup of sugar and 1/8 teaspoon of salt.
2. Stir until thoroughly blended.
3. Take butter and place on top of flour mixture.
4. Push butter into mixture with fingers.
5. Work the butter into the flour mixture to form a coarse meal.
6. Make a well in the coarse meal by pushing a ½ cup measuring cup into the center of the coarse meal.
7. Make sure to leave a dent in the middle of dough.
8. Break egg into the well.
9. Add the lemon juice. Stir.
10. Knead the flour into the egg to form soft dough.
11. Make sure dough is well blended.

12. Shape into a pie disk and chill in the freezer for 60 minutes.

Final steps

1. Heat oven at 400 degrees F. Place flour on a flat cooking surface.
2. Use roller to flatten pie dough.
3. Press the pie pastry into the prepped pie pan.
4. Bake until golden brown for 12 to 15 minutes.
5. Take out of oven and let cool for 15 minutes.
6. In a medium bowl, mix cream cheese, powdered sugar and peanut butter together until smooth.
7. Fold in ½ cup of the whipped cream.
8. Spoon the mixture into the piecrust.
9. Cover.
10. Chill overnight before serving.
11. Serve with whipped cream.
12. Enjoy!

Before you go, I'd like to remind you that there is a free, complimentary eBook waiting for you. Download it today to treat yourself to healthy, <u>gluten-free desserts and snacks</u> so that you never feel deprived again!

Download link

<u>http://bit.ly/gluten-free-desserts-book</u>

Conclusion

So, how was your baking party?

Did you enjoy my recipes?

Remember that you can always create your own healthier variations. For example, coconut oil can substitute butter and coconut cream or plain Greek yoghurt can substitute all kinds of creams. Feel free to experiment and choose what you and your family like.

Herbs and spices are an excellent way to spice up your baking. You can also add cinnamon, nutmeg and ginger to your smoothies and juices, your body will be utterly grateful!

Preparation is the key to success. If you are on a busy schedule (like me and my family) make sure you do your gluten-free baking on the weekends. It's a great way to socialize with your family and friends. You can also get them involved.

Final words: While the gluten-free diet is a medical treatment for individuals with celiac disease or gluten intolerance, it can be beneficial for nearly everyone. Before you decide whether the gluten-free diet is the right choice for you, take the time to learn as much as you can about the diet including its benefits, its risks, and which foods you can and cannot eat.

If you decide that the gluten-free diet is the diet for you, I hope you will try some of the recipes in this book as you transition into the diet. Please let me know your favorites- the review section of this book is an excellent place to share your experience with other readers.

To post an honest review

One more thing... If you have received any value from this book, can you please rank it and post a short review? It only takes a few seconds really and it would really make my day. It's you I am writing for and your opinion is always much appreciated. In order to do so;

1. Log into your account
2. Search for my book on Amazon or check your orders/ or go to my author page at:

http://amazon.com/author/kira-novac

3. Click on a book you have read, then click on "reviews" and "create your review".

Please let me know your favorite motivational tip you learned from this book.

I would love to hear from you!

If you happen to have any questions or doubts about this book, please e-mail me at:

kira.novac@kiraglutenfreerecipes.com

I am here to help!

Recommended Reading

Book Link:

http://bit.ly/vegan-gf-baking

Recommended Reading

Book Link:

http://bit.ly/anti-inflammatory-recipes

FOR MORE HEALTH BOOKS (KINDLE & PAPERBACK) BY KIRA NOVAC PLEASE VISIT:

www.kiraglutenfreerecipes.com/books

Thank you for taking an interest in my work,

Kira and Holistic Wellness Books

HOLISTIC WELLNESS & HEALTH BOOKS

If you are interested in health, wellness, spirituality and personal development, visit our page and be the first one to know about free and 0.99 eBooks:

www.HolisticWellnessBooks.com